365

ways

to say

THANK YOU

Bella S.

ISBN: **1491238348**
ISBN-13: **978-1491238349**

DEDICATION

While I am the moon, this book is dedicated to my sun.

This book is the first one in the series of 365 days, 365 ways.

Enjoy browse through it.

Congratulations! Today is the first day of the best year of your life so far. A year in front of you has 365 days. Turn one page of this book every day and write down one way to say THANK YOU then read through aloud.

At the end of the year you may have your very own 365 ways to say THANK YOU by heart.

On this page write down one way to say
THANK YOU,
You used or You will use today.

On this page write down one way to say
THANK YOU,
You used or You will use today.

On this page write down one way to say
THANK YOU,
You used or You will use today.

On this page write down one way to say
THANK YOU,
You used or You will use today.

On this page write down one way to say
THANK YOU,
You used or You will use today.

On this page write down one way to say
THANK YOU,
You used or You will use today.

On this page write down one way to say
THANK YOU,
You used or You will use today.

On this page write down one way to say
THANK YOU,
You used or You will use today.

On this page write down one way to say
THANK YOU,
You used or You will use today.

On this page write down one way to say
THANK YOU,
You used or You will use today.

On this page write down one way to say
THANK YOU,
You used or You will use today.

On this page write down one way to say
THANK YOU,
You used or You will use today.

On this page write down one way to say
THANK YOU,
You used or You will use today.

On this page write down one way to say
THANK YOU,
You used or You will use today.

On this page write down one way to say
THANK YOU,
You used or You will use today.

On this page write down one way to say
THANK YOU,
You used or You will use today.

On this page write down one way to say
THANK YOU,
You used or You will use today.

On this page write down one way to say
THANK YOU,
You used or You will use today.

On this page write down one way to say
THANK YOU,
You used or You will use today.

On this page write down one way to say
THANK YOU,
You used or You will use today.

On this page write down one way to say
THANK YOU,
You used or You will use today.

On this page write down one way to say
THANK YOU,
You used or You will use today.

On this page write down one way to say
THANK YOU,
You used or You will use today.

On this page write down one way to say
THANK YOU,
You used or You will use today.

On this page write down one way to say
THANK YOU,
You used or You will use today.

On this page write down one way to say
THANK YOU,
You used or You will use today.

On this page write down one way to say
THANK YOU,
You used or You will use today.

On this page write down one way to say
THANK YOU,
You used or You will use today.

On this page write down one way to say
THANK YOU,
You used or You will use today.

On this page write down one way to say
THANK YOU,
You used or You will use today.

On this page write down one way to say
THANK YOU,
You used or You will use today.

On this page write down one way to say
THANK YOU,
You used or You will use today.

On this page write down one way to say
THANK YOU,
You used or You will use today.

On this page write down one way to say
THANK YOU,
You used or You will use today.

On this page write down one way to say
THANK YOU,
You used or You will use today.

On this page write down one way to say
THANK YOU,
You used or You will use today.

On this page write down one way to say
THANK YOU,
You used or You will use today.

On this page write down one way to say
THANK YOU,
You used or You will use today.

On this page write down one way to say
THANK YOU,
You used or You will use today.

On this page write down one way to say
THANK YOU,
You used or You will use today.

On this page write down one way to say
THANK YOU,
You used or You will use today.

On this page write down one way to say
THANK YOU,
You used or You will use today.

On this page write down one way to say
THANK YOU,
You used or You will use today.

On this page write down one way to say
THANK YOU,
You used or You will use today.

On this page write down one way to say
THANK YOU,
You used or You will use today.

On this page write down one way to say
THANK YOU,
You used or You will use today.

On this page write down one way to say
THANK YOU,
You used or You will use today.

On this page write down one way to say
THANK YOU,
You used or You will use today.

On this page write down one way to say
THANK YOU,
You used or You will use today.

On this page write down one way to say
THANK YOU,
You used or You will use today.

On this page write down one way to say
THANK YOU,
You used or You will use today.

On this page write down one way to say
THANK YOU,
You used or You will use today.

On this page write down one way to say
THANK YOU,
You used or You will use today.

On this page write down one way to say
THANK YOU,
You used or You will use today.

On this page write down one way to say
THANK YOU,
You used or You will use today.

On this page write down one way to say
THANK YOU,
You used or You will use today.

On this page write down one way to say
THANK YOU,
You used or You will use today.

On this page write down one way to say
THANK YOU,
You used or You will use today.

On this page write down one way to say
THANK YOU,
You used or You will use today.

On this page write down one way to say
THANK YOU,
You used or You will use today.

On this page write down one way to say
THANK YOU,
You used or You will use today.

On this page write down one way to say
THANK YOU,
You used or You will use today.

On this page write down one way to say
THANK YOU,
You used or You will use today.

On this page write down one way to say
THANK YOU,
You used or You will use today.

On this page write down one way to say
THANK YOU,
You used or You will use today.

On this page write down one way to say
THANK YOU,
You used or You will use today.

On this page write down one way to say
THANK YOU,
You used or You will use today.

On this page write down one way to say
THANK YOU,
You used or You will use today.

On this page write down one way to say
THANK YOU,
You used or You will use today.

On this page write down one way to say
THANK YOU,
You used or You will use today.

On this page write down one way to say
THANK YOU,
You used or You will use today.

On this page write down one way to say
THANK YOU,
You used or You will use today.

On this page write down one way to say
THANK YOU,
You used or You will use today.

On this page write down one way to say
THANK YOU,
You used or You will use today.

On this page write down one way to say
THANK YOU,
You used or You will use today.

On this page write down one way to say
THANK YOU,
You used or You will use today.

On this page write down one way to say
THANK YOU,
You used or You will use today.

On this page write down one way to say
THANK YOU,
You used or You will use today.

On this page write down one way to say
THANK YOU,
You used or You will use today.

On this page write down one way to say
THANK YOU,
You used or You will use today.

On this page write down one way to say
THANK YOU,
You used or You will use today.

365 ways to say THANK YOU

On this page write down one way to say
THANK YOU,
You used or You will use today.

On this page write down one way to say
THANK YOU,
You used or You will use today.

On this page write down one way to say
THANK YOU,
You used or You will use today.

On this page write down one way to say
THANK YOU,
You used or You will use today.

On this page write down one way to say
THANK YOU,
You used or You will use today.

On this page write down one way to say
THANK YOU,
You used or You will use today.

On this page write down one way to say
THANK YOU,
You used or You will use today.

On this page write down one way to say
THANK YOU,
You used or You will use today.

On this page write down one way to say
THANK YOU,
You used or You will use today.

On this page write down one way to say
THANK YOU,
You used or You will use today.

On this page write down one way to say
THANK YOU,
You used or You will use today.

On this page write down one way to say
THANK YOU,
You used or You will use today.

On this page write down one way to say
THANK YOU,
You used or You will use today.

On this page write down one way to say
THANK YOU,
You used or You will use today.

On this page write down one way to say
THANK YOU,
You used or You will use today.

On this page write down one way to say
THANK YOU,
You used or You will use today.

On this page write down one way to say
THANK YOU,
You used or You will use today.

On this page write down one way to say
THANK YOU,
You used or You will use today.

On this page write down one way to say
THANK YOU,
You used or You will use today.

On this page write down one way to say
THANK YOU,
You used or You will use today.

On this page write down one way to say
THANK YOU,
You used or You will use today.

On this page write down one way to say
THANK YOU,
You used or You will use today.

On this page write down one way to say
THANK YOU,
You used or You will use today.

On this page write down one way to say
THANK YOU,
You used or You will use today.

On this page write down one way to say
THANK YOU,
You used or You will use today.

On this page write down one way to say
THANK YOU,
You used or You will use today.

On this page write down one way to say
THANK YOU,
You used or You will use today.

On this page write down one way to say
THANK YOU,
You used or You will use today.

On this page write down one way to say
THANK YOU,
You used or You will use today.

On this page write down one way to say
THANK YOU,
You used or You will use today.

On this page write down one way to say
THANK YOU,
You used or You will use today.

On this page write down one way to say
THANK YOU,
You used or You will use today.

On this page write down one way to say
THANK YOU,
You used or You will use today.

On this page write down one way to say
THANK YOU,
You used or You will use today.

On this page write down one way to say
THANK YOU,
You used or You will use today.

On this page write down one way to say
THANK YOU,
You used or You will use today.

On this page write down one way to say
THANK YOU,
You used or You will use today.

On this page write down one way to say
THANK YOU,
You used or You will use today.

On this page write down one way to say
THANK YOU,
You used or You will use today.

On this page write down one way to say
THANK YOU,
You used or You will use today.

On this page write down one way to say
THANK YOU,
You used or You will use today.

On this page write down one way to say
THANK YOU,
You used or You will use today.

On this page write down one way to say
THANK YOU,
You used or You will use today.

On this page write down one way to say
THANK YOU,
You used or You will use today.

On this page write down one way to say
THANK YOU,
You used or You will use today.

On this page write down one way to say
THANK YOU,
You used or You will use today.

On this page write down one way to say
THANK YOU,
You used or You will use today.

On this page write down one way to say
THANK YOU,
You used or You will use today.

On this page write down one way to say
THANK YOU,
You used or You will use today.

On this page write down one way to say
THANK YOU,
You used or You will use today.

On this page write down one way to say
THANK YOU,
You used or You will use today.

On this page write down one way to say
THANK YOU,
You used or You will use today.

On this page write down one way to say
THANK YOU,
You used or You will use today.

On this page write down one way to say
THANK YOU,
You used or You will use today.

On this page write down one way to say
THANK YOU,
You used or You will use today.

On this page write down one way to say
THANK YOU,
You used or You will use today.

On this page write down one way to say
THANK YOU,
You used or You will use today.

On this page write down one way to say
THANK YOU,
You used or You will use today.

On this page write down one way to say
THANK YOU,
You used or You will use today.

On this page write down one way to say
THANK YOU,
You used or You will use today.

On this page write down one way to say
THANK YOU,
You used or You will use today.

On this page write down one way to say
THANK YOU,
You used or You will use today.

On this page write down one way to say
THANK YOU,
You used or You will use today.

On this page write down one way to say
THANK YOU,
You used or You will use today.

On this page write down one way to say
THANK YOU,
You used or You will use today.

On this page write down one way to say
THANK YOU,
You used or You will use today.

On this page write down one way to say
THANK YOU,
You used or You will use today.

On this page write down one way to say
THANK YOU,
You used or You will use today.

On this page write down one way to say
THANK YOU,
You used or You will use today.

On this page write down one way to say
THANK YOU,
You used or You will use today.

On this page write down one way to say
THANK YOU,
You used or You will use today.

On this page write down one way to say
THANK YOU,
You used or You will use today.

On this page write down one way to say
THANK YOU,
You used or You will use today.

On this page write down one way to say
THANK YOU,
You used or You will use today.

On this page write down one way to say
THANK YOU,
You used or You will use today.

On this page write down one way to say
THANK YOU,
You used or You will use today.

On this page write down one way to say
THANK YOU,
You used or You will use today.

On this page write down one way to say
THANK YOU,
You used or You will use today.

On this page write down one way to say
THANK YOU,
You used or You will use today.

On this page write down one way to say
THANK YOU,
You used or You will use today.

On this page write down one way to say
THANK YOU,
You used or You will use today.

On this page write down one way to say
THANK YOU,
You used or You will use today.

On this page write down one way to say
THANK YOU,
You used or You will use today.

On this page write down one way to say
THANK YOU,
You used or You will use today.

On this page write down one way to say
THANK YOU,
You used or You will use today.

On this page write down one way to say
THANK YOU,
You used or You will use today.

167

On this page write down one way to say
THANK YOU,
You used or You will use today.

On this page write down one way to say
THANK YOU,
You used or You will use today.

On this page write down one way to say
THANK YOU,
You used or You will use today.

On this page write down one way to say
THANK YOU,
You used or You will use today.

On this page write down one way to say
THANK YOU,
You used or You will use today.

On this page write down one way to say
THANK YOU,
You used or You will use today.

On this page write down one way to say
THANK YOU,
You used or You will use today.

On this page write down one way to say
THANK YOU,
You used or You will use today.

On this page write down one way to say
THANK YOU,
You used or You will use today.

On this page write down one way to say
THANK YOU,
You used or You will use today.

On this page write down one way to say
THANK YOU,
You used or You will use today.

On this page write down one way to say
THANK YOU,
You used or You will use today.

On this page write down one way to say
THANK YOU,
You used or You will use today.

On this page write down one way to say
THANK YOU,
You used or You will use today.

On this page write down one way to say
THANK YOU,
You used or You will use today.

On this page write down one way to say
THANK YOU,
You used or You will use today.

On this page write down one way to say
THANK YOU,
You used or You will use today.

On this page write down one way to say
THANK YOU,
You used or You will use today.

On this page write down one way to say
THANK YOU,
You used or You will use today.

On this page write down one way to say
THANK YOU,
You used or You will use today.

On this page write down one way to say
THANK YOU,
You used or You will use today.

On this page write down one way to say
THANK YOU,
You used or You will use today.

On this page write down one way to say
THANK YOU,
You used or You will use today.

On this page write down one way to say
THANK YOU,
You used or You will use today.

On this page write down one way to say
THANK YOU,
You used or You will use today.

On this page write down one way to say
THANK YOU,
You used or You will use today.

On this page write down one way to say
THANK YOU,
You used or You will use today.

On this page write down one way to say
THANK YOU,
You used or You will use today.

On this page write down one way to say
THANK YOU,
You used or You will use today.

On this page write down one way to say
THANK YOU,
You used or You will use today.

On this page write down one way to say
THANK YOU,
You used or You will use today.

On this page write down one way to say
THANK YOU,
You used or You will use today.

On this page write down one way to say
THANK YOU,
You used or You will use today.

On this page write down one way to say
THANK YOU,
You used or You will use today.

On this page write down one way to say
THANK YOU,
You used or You will use today.

On this page write down one way to say
THANK YOU,
You used or You will use today.

On this page write down one way to say
THANK YOU,
You used or You will use today.

On this page write down one way to say
THANK YOU,
You used or You will use today.

On this page write down one way to say
THANK YOU,
You used or You will use today.

On this page write down one way to say
THANK YOU,
You used or You will use today.

On this page write down one way to say
THANK YOU,
You used or You will use today.

On this page write down one way to say
THANK YOU,
You used or You will use today.

On this page write down one way to say
THANK YOU,
You used or You will use today.

On this page write down one way to say
THANK YOU,
You used or You will use today.

On this page write down one way to say
THANK YOU,
You used or You will use today.

On this page write down one way to say
THANK YOU,
You used or You will use today.

On this page write down one way to say
THANK YOU,
You used or You will use today.

On this page write down one way to say
THANK YOU,
You used or You will use today.

On this page write down one way to say
THANK YOU,
You used or You will use today.

On this page write down one way to say
THANK YOU,
You used or You will use today.

On this page write down one way to say
THANK YOU,
You used or You will use today.

On this page write down one way to say
THANK YOU,
You used or You will use today.

On this page write down one way to say
THANK YOU,
You used or You will use today.

On this page write down one way to say
THANK YOU,
You used or You will use today.

On this page write down one way to say
THANK YOU,
You used or You will use today.

On this page write down one way to say
THANK YOU,
You used or You will use today.

On this page write down one way to say
THANK YOU,
You used or You will use today.

On this page write down one way to say
THANK YOU,
You used or You will use today.

On this page write down one way to say
THANK YOU,
You used or You will use today.

On this page write down one way to say
THANK YOU,
You used or You will use today.

On this page write down one way to say
THANK YOU,
You used or You will use today.

On this page write down one way to say
THANK YOU,
You used or You will use today.

On this page write down one way to say
THANK YOU,
You used or You will use today.

On this page write down one way to say
THANK YOU,
You used or You will use today.

On this page write down one way to say
THANK YOU,
You used or You will use today.

On this page write down one way to say
THANK YOU,
You used or You will use today.

On this page write down one way to say
THANK YOU,
You used or You will use today.

On this page write down one way to say
THANK YOU,
You used or You will use today.

On this page write down one way to say
THANK YOU,
You used or You will use today.

On this page write down one way to say
THANK YOU,
You used or You will use today.

On this page write down one way to say
THANK YOU,
You used or You will use today.

On this page write down one way to say
THANK YOU,
You used or You will use today.

On this page write down one way to say
THANK YOU,
You used or You will use today.

On this page write down one way to say
THANK YOU,
You used or You will use today.

On this page write down one way to say
THANK YOU,
You used or You will use today.

On this page write down one way to say
THANK YOU,
You used or You will use today.

On this page write down one way to say
THANK YOU,
You used or You will use today.

On this page write down one way to say
THANK YOU,
You used or You will use today.

On this page write down one way to say
THANK YOU,
You used or You will use today.

On this page write down one way to say
THANK YOU,
You used or You will use today.

On this page write down one way to say
THANK YOU,
You used or You will use today.

On this page write down one way to say
THANK YOU,
You used or You will use today.

On this page write down one way to say
THANK YOU,
You used or You will use today.

250

On this page write down one way to say
THANK YOU,
You used or You will use today.

On this page write down one way to say
THANK YOU,
You used or You will use today.

On this page write down one way to say
THANK YOU,
You used or You will use today.

On this page write down one way to say
THANK YOU,
You used or You will use today.

On this page write down one way to say
THANK YOU,
You used or You will use today.

On this page write down one way to say
THANK YOU,
You used or You will use today.

On this page write down one way to say
THANK YOU,
You used or You will use today.

On this page write down one way to say
THANK YOU,
You used or You will use today.

On this page write down one way to say
THANK YOU,
You used or You will use today.

On this page write down one way to say
THANK YOU,
You used or You will use today.

On this page write down one way to say
THANK YOU,
You used or You will use today.

On this page write down one way to say
THANK YOU,
You used or You will use today.

On this page write down one way to say
THANK YOU,
You used or You will use today.

On this page write down one way to say
THANK YOU,
You used or You will use today.

On this page write down one way to say
THANK YOU,
You used or You will use today.

On this page write down one way to say
THANK YOU,
You used or You will use today.

On this page write down one way to say
THANK YOU,
You used or You will use today.

On this page write down one way to say
THANK YOU,
You used or You will use today.

On this page write down one way to say
THANK YOU,
You used or You will use today.

On this page write down one way to say
THANK YOU,
You used or You will use today.

On this page write down one way to say
THANK YOU,
You used or You will use today.

On this page write down one way to say
THANK YOU,
You used or You will use today.

On this page write down one way to say
THANK YOU,
You used or You will use today.

On this page write down one way to say
THANK YOU,
You used or You will use today.

On this page write down one way to say
THANK YOU,
You used or You will use today.

On this page write down one way to say
THANK YOU,
You used or You will use today.

On this page write down one way to say
THANK YOU,
You used or You will use today.

On this page write down one way to say
THANK YOU,
You used or You will use today.

On this page write down one way to say
THANK YOU,
You used or You will use today.

On this page write down one way to say
THANK YOU,
You used or You will use today.

On this page write down one way to say
THANK YOU,
You used or You will use today.

On this page write down one way to say
THANK YOU,
You used or You will use today.

On this page write down one way to say
THANK YOU,
You used or You will use today.

On this page write down one way to say
THANK YOU,
You used or You will use today.

On this page write down one way to say
THANK YOU,
You used or You will use today.

On this page write down one way to say
THANK YOU,
You used or You will use today.

On this page write down one way to say
THANK YOU,
You used or You will use today.

On this page write down one way to say
THANK YOU,
You used or You will use today.

On this page write down one way to say
THANK YOU,
You used or You will use today.

On this page write down one way to say
THANK YOU,
You used or You will use today.

On this page write down one way to say
THANK YOU,
You used or You will use today.

On this page write down one way to say
THANK YOU,
You used or You will use today.

On this page write down one way to say
THANK YOU,
You used or You will use today.

On this page write down one way to say
THANK YOU,
You used or You will use today.

On this page write down one way to say
THANK YOU,
You used or You will use today.

On this page write down one way to say
THANK YOU,
You used or You will use today.

On this page write down one way to say
THANK YOU,
You used or You will use today.

On this page write down one way to say
THANK YOU,
You used or You will use today.

On this page write down one way to say
THANK YOU,
You used or You will use today.

On this page write down one way to say
THANK YOU,
You used or You will use today.

On this page write down one way to say
THANK YOU,
You used or You will use today.

On this page write down one way to say
THANK YOU,
You used or You will use today.

On this page write down one way to say
THANK YOU,
You used or You will use today.

On this page write down one way to say
THANK YOU,
You used or You will use today.

On this page write down one way to say
THANK YOU,
You used or You will use today.

On this page write down one way to say
THANK YOU,
You used or You will use today.

On this page write down one way to say
THANK YOU,
You used or You will use today.

On this page write down one way to say
THANK YOU,
You used or You will use today.

On this page write down one way to say
THANK YOU,
You used or You will use today.

On this page write down one way to say
THANK YOU,
You used or You will use today.

On this page write down one way to say
THANK YOU,
You used or You will use today.

On this page write down one way to say
THANK YOU,
You used or You will use today.

On this page write down one way to say
THANK YOU,
You used or You will use today.

On this page write down one way to say
THANK YOU,
You used or You will use today.

On this page write down one way to say
THANK YOU,
You used or You will use today.

On this page write down one way to say
THANK YOU,
You used or You will use today.

On this page write down one way to say
THANK YOU,
You used or You will use today.

On this page write down one way to say
THANK YOU,
You used or You will use today.

On this page write down one way to say
THANK YOU,
You used or You will use today.

On this page write down one way to say
THANK YOU,
You used or You will use today.

On this page write down one way to say
THANK YOU,
You used or You will use today.

On this page write down one way to say
THANK YOU,
You used or You will use today.

On this page write down one way to say
THANK YOU,
You used or You will use today.

On this page write down one way to say
THANK YOU,
You used or You will use today.

On this page write down one way to say
THANK YOU,
You used or You will use today.

On this page write down one way to say
THANK YOU,
You used or You will use today.

On this page write down one way to say
THANK YOU,
You used or You will use today.

On this page write down one way to say
THANK YOU,
You used or You will use today.

On this page write down one way to say
THANK YOU,
You used or You will use today.

On this page write down one way to say
THANK YOU,
You used or You will use today.

On this page write down one way to say
THANK YOU,
You used or You will use today.

On this page write down one way to say
THANK YOU,
You used or You will use today.

On this page write down one way to say
THANK YOU,
You used or You will use today.

On this page write down one way to say
THANK YOU,
You used or You will use today.

On this page write down one way to say
THANK YOU,
You used or You will use today.

On this page write down one way to say
THANK YOU,
You used or You will use today.

On this page write down one way to say
THANK YOU,
You used or You will use today.

On this page write down one way to say
THANK YOU,
You used or You will use today.

On this page write down one way to say
THANK YOU,
You used or You will use today.

On this page write down one way to say
THANK YOU,
You used or You will use today.

On this page write down one way to say
THANK YOU,
You used or You will use today.

On this page write down one way to say
THANK YOU,
You used or You will use today.

On this page write down one way to say
THANK YOU,
You used or You will use today.

On this page write down one way to say
THANK YOU,
You used or You will use today.

On this page write down one way to say
THANK YOU,
You used or You will use today.

On this page write down one way to say
THANK YOU,
You used or You will use today.

On this page write down one way to say
THANK YOU,
You used or You will use today.

On this page write down one way to say
THANK YOU,
You used or You will use today.

On this page write down one way to say
THANK YOU,
You used or You will use today.

On this page write down one way to say
THANK YOU,
You used or You will use today.

On this page write down one way to say
THANK YOU,
You used or You will use today.

On this page write down one way to say
THANK YOU,
You used or You will use today.

On this page write down one way to say
THANK YOU,
You used or You will use today.

On this page write down one way to say
THANK YOU,
You used or You will use today.

On this page write down one way to say
THANK YOU,
You used or You will use today.

On this page write down one way to say
THANK YOU,
You used or You will use today.

On this page write down one way to say
THANK YOU,
You used or You will use today.

On this page write down one way to say
THANK YOU,
You used or You will use today.

On this page write down one way to say
THANK YOU,
You used or You will use today.

On this page write down one way to say
THANK YOU,
You used or You will use today.

On this page write down one way to say
THANK YOU,
You used or You will use today.

On this page write down one way to say
THANK YOU,
You used or You will use today.

On this page write down one way to say
THANK YOU,
You used or You will use today.

On this page write down one way to say
THANK YOU,
You used or You will use today.

365 ways to say THANK YOU

On this page write down one way to say
THANK YOU,
You used or You will use today.

A year has gone by since you started reading this book. Now, look back and 'connect the dots' to see the changes that happened in your life.

Thank you for reading this book. Wish you all the best.

10q

Made in the USA
San Bernardino, CA
22 December 2016